AF255595

CHICKEN HAIKU

CHICKEN HAIKU

Poems by Karin S. Wiberg

Illustrations by Dawn Marie Rozzo

CLEAR SIGHT BOOKS

Raleigh, North Carolina

2018

Published by Clear Sight Books, Raleigh, North Carolina
First edition: December 2018

ISBN: 978-1-945209-05-5 (hardback)
ISBN: 978-1-945209-04-8 (paperback)
Library of Congress Control Number: 2018913159

For more information, visit chickenhaiku.com.

Introduction

A Note about Our Chickens

In 2011, my husband and I went on our first "Tour D'Coop" in Raleigh, North Carolina—an annual event where backyard chicken owners welcome curious visitors. The idea of having a chicken flock in our urban backyard intrigued us.

Over the next year we did research, built a coop, and acquired our first three hens: Victoria, a Salmon Faverolles, and Margaret and Anne, Black Australorps. Since then, we've lost Victoria and Anne and added Charlotte and Eleanor, Speckled Sussex, Isabella, an Ameraucana, and Ermengarde, a Barnevelder.

Not only do we get yummy eggs from the ladies, but they are terribly entertaining; "Chickenpapa" and I spend many evenings watching them free-range in the backyard. A few of the ladies make an appearance in this book, and the art reflects their personality, if not always their breed.

I find chickens the perfect subjects for haiku.

—KSW

An Invitation to Haiku

Growing up, many of us learned one rule about the Japanese poetry form *haiku*: it has three lines with syllable counts of 5-7-5. That "rule" is something of an overly simplified translation. Haiku are indeed short, and a three-line structure is common in English-language haiku, but a precise line or syllable count tends to be less important than observing some of the broader principles.

As part of their brevity, haiku capture a moment in time. Unlike many other poetic forms, haiku tend not to use overt metaphor. Rather, they usually work by placing two images side by side. The juxtaposition creates an interesting tension or an enhanced layer of meaning.

Japanese haiku use a *kireji*, sometimes translated as "cutting word," to create a pause that indicates the pivot between images or that brings resonance at the end of the poem. In English there's no direct equivalent; a kireji is often represented as punctuation, such as a dash or an ellipsis.

Haiku are often about nature and usually contain a *kigo*, or "season word." For example, in my poems, "wind blusters" indicates early spring; "unexpected rink" signifies winter.

Most English-language haiku do not rhyme, but early in my haiku-writing experience I read my grandmother's copy of Harold G. Henderson's 1958 book *An Introduction to Haiku*, in which the author translates many classic haiku using rhyme. The style grew on me, so rhyme does pop up in several of my poems.

Haiku are so short they don't have titles, and when you read one aloud, it's common to read the haiku once, pause, and then read it again.

As a writer, I appreciate the principles of haiku and love all the subtleties of the form. But I encourage you not to get too stuck on "rules." Just enjoy reading these chicken haiku alongside their delightful illustrations by my feather-loving collaborator, Dawn.

—KSW

The Interplay of Arts

When Karin first floated the idea of illustrating her chicken haiku, my immediate thought was *Yes!* Creating art within her framework of beautiful poems made visual decision-making a pleasure.

I work in pencil, watercolor, acrylics, and collage. My collages contain hand-made papers and/or papers reassembled from discarded books, which are then prepared with clear gesso for painting. I appreciated the irony of using disassembled books to create illustrations for a new book.

For most of the chicken images here, I created illustrations to match Karin's poems. However, a few times Karin saw my art and then wrote complementary haiku. It was fascinating to see how the two art forms played off each other.

Enjoy!

—DMR

Grapes
ries

Matrons take a break

from egg-laying duties—

morning kaffeeklatsch.

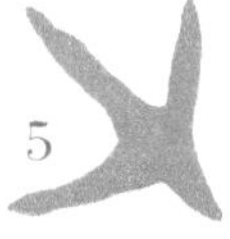

Wind blusters,

    chickens in their bloomers—

        feather dusters!

Three hens huddle

underneath the dripping roost—

stones in a puddle.

Scratch, scratch, scratch,

digging for gold flecks—

when do dreams hatch?

 10

A BIRD'S EYE VIEW
OF THE
OF MUSIC,
JOHN

GENETICS
143
all albinos belong ... same genotype
All individuals w... ...rmal pigmentation
two alleles of ... belong to th... ...e but may be of
In symbolizing ... either the hom... ...genotype AA or the
capitalize the gene sym... ...trait heterozy... ...ype Aa. The complete
and put its recessive part... in small haploid (monoploid) set of chromosomes char-
letters. For example, a sym... recessive acteristic of the cells of any individual consti-
gene for albinism ... ...responding tutes that individual's genome. In other words

Downy brood

in a warm milieu—

as if on cue, we coo.

Speckled Sussex

flashes white-dappled feathers—

dogwood petals in sun.

scena delle prodezz… governo di Salom… Ger. 47: 1, 5; m… 2: 4; Zacc. 9: 5; è … 26. Era una delle precip… santuario del dio Marn… distrutti l'anno 400 … Arabi, 634; ristaurata… Saladino, 1170, e di n… Conta ora 18,000 (luogo calpestato, aia), antico nome città giace in … Cananei, Giud. 19: 10, 11 (Iebus); e di porte. … probabilmente derivato da un discen- sul colle … glio di Cam, Gen. 10: 16. I Gebusei moder… parte sottomessi da Giosuè, Gios. 10: 23, 40; … 15: 63; Num. 13: 22; ma Davide permise loro di … rare in Gebus dopo la sua conquista, 2 Sam. 5: 6-9; 24: 16-25; 1 Cron. 11: 4-8, Esd. 9: … spondeva esattamente al colle … Sion o Città di Davide. Circondat… fondi burron…

Gebuse… attorno a … che … 20: 17. Adonis… dipoi … riabita… prese q… sua capit… li lasciò s… 1 Re 9: 20… ni d… possono rintracciare anche dopo la cattività, Esd. 9: 1. Davide comprò per erigervi un altare, l'aia di Arauna Gebuseo. Più tardi Salomone vi edificò il tempio, 2 Sam. 24: 16-25.

Geconia (che Geova stabilisce), Vedi GIOIACHIN.

Gedeone (tagliatore d'alberi), figlio di Ioas Abi- zerita e quinto giudice d'Israele. Ci si presenta la prima … a quando un angelo gli appare sotto la quercia di … e gli promette il favore di Dio, Giud. 6: 11, 12. In seguito, Dio gli ordinò di offrire, come sacrificio al Si- gnore, il giovenco che suo padre avea messo da parte per Baal, e di distruggere l'altare di quella falsa divi- nità. Egli ubbidì; ma, senza l'accorto intervento del padre, sarebbe caduto vittima del furore de' suoi con- cittadini, Giud. 6…

Le grandi ope… Gedeone furono l'abolizione del- l'idolatria, Giud. … e la liberazione del paese dalle mani dei Madianit… Prima di intraprendere quest'ul- tima, chiese ed ottenne due pegni del favore di Dio, i prodigi della rugiada e del vello, Giud. 6: 36-40. Vo- lendo Dio che chiaramente apparisse non esser la vitto- ria dovuta agli uomini, ma ad intervento soprannatu- rale, egli ridusse l'esercito di Gedeone da 32,000 a 300. Co… manipolo, e a mezzo dello stratagemma delle … nei testi e delle trombe, Gedeone spar- … ranghi nemici e gli sbaragliò, Giud. 7.

THE END
his bed was re…
Polish chaplain.
'Don't forget to let them …
… the fish mar…

Gelosia, Cappella dell'idolo di, E… lo stesso che Tammuz nel v. 14. Vedi TAM… **Gelosia, Offerta di acqua di.** Vedi… **Gelsi.** Tutti son d'accordo nel ripudiar…

Peeps climb

on grass-nestled mama—

backyard jungle gym.

Into the world for the first time, teenage chickens discover crickets.

18

Visiting toddler

touches prehistoric feet—

leaps back just in time.

Hens wade in weeds,

eat flowers and seeds.

Smell of gasoline.

22

FIGURE 75. *Capsella bursa-pastoris* (L) Medic. 1, habit; 2, undersurface of leaf; 3, flower; 4, fruit or seedpod (silique); 5, seed, two views; 6, seedlings.

Startled by a squirrel,

   Isabella flaps in circles—

      Chicken Little's sky.

25

Five hens preen

    on patio-chair perches—

        Saturday night dance.

WHEN ORDERING PLEASE STATE THE LENGTH OF SKIRT

Margaret dunks dirt

till black feathers shimmer—

blue satin ball gown.

Chickens strut their stuff

    around the yard, atop the cage—

        all the world's a stage!

30

60
22.—ТЕАТР
1. Театр.
2. Актер.
3. Актриса.
4. Зритель.
5. Галлерея, галерка.
6. Ложа.
7. Место.
8. Место за креслами, амфитеатр партера.
9. Кресла партера и пар-
10.
11.
CATHERINE
vez-vous fait
lui comme
Le mari et
ttent à danser
les trois

Chickens dig,

earthworms zig . . . too slow!

It's time to eat.

On sunny pavement

Annabel lies, wings splayed—

half-baked chicken.

34

Hens eat watermelon—

Charlotte wipes her beak on Chickenpapa.

Golden-hour specks

dance over grazing hens.

Shadows stretch.

INTERRUPTED BROKEN CADENCE.
instead of introducing a *final* or *false cadence* we may make a
instead of the tonic, as in the following after which we
already recommended
after the dominant, placin
proceed as pointed out at

Secure behind wire

chickens warble at dusk—

sunset fire.

Two black chickens hide in shadow—

sunlight lost each day.

 42

Feathers in yard,

chickens cringe from touch—

prick of new growth.

Ramp closes,

    shuffle in the roost—

        moon poses.

46

THE ANIMAL AND ITS ENVIRONMENT   691
overgrazed and the other lightly
figures indicate their relative abun
sweeps of the insect net, each.
a period of a month and indicate a very
t populations of the two areas
is attained and cottonwoods give way to oaks and
elms, of the insects to be found in each
stage of development After the name of each insect
is
Seasonal Changes
n observation that the animals observed
eatl from season to season during the
Fly
Heterocerus
Beetle (tritus)
Bembidion
Beetle (detritus)
Cicindela
Tiger
Cicindela
Tiger Beetle (small insect)
Cicindela punctulata
Tiger Beetle (small insects)
Mutillidae
Velvet ants (insects and spiders)
Apion pennsylvanicum
Weevil (cocklebur)
Haltica bimarginata
Beetle (willow)
Phalacrus politus
Beetle (willow)
Stictocephala lutea
Tree hopper (willow, cottonwood)
Cicadella gothica
Leafhopper (willow)
D tomus squamosus
W vil (willow)
Strongylocornis stygicus
Bug (coral berry)
Epitrix brevis
Flea Beetle (Miscellaneous plants)
Brief descriptions of stages:
    1. Mud flat with blue-green algae, later
    2. Sedges, willow and cottonwood seedlings
    3. Second level. Sand, sedges, willows, c
    4. Third level. Grasses, willows, cotton
    5. Third level. Cottonwoods, fewer willows
    6. Fourth level. Elm-oak forest
    *x indicates the presence of
munity.
average catch with 100 sweeps of an
homa) arranged according to orders
n Carpenter.)

Unexpected rink—

novice ice-skater lands

a flying sit spin.

Silent night,

hens tucked in—

starlight on snow.

50

The End

Victoria—our first

About the Illustrator

Dawn Marie Rozzo's paintings can be found in private collections across the United States. When Dawn isn't in the studio, she's working in her flower garden accompanied by her two nosey cats. Her lifelong love of nature informs her semi-abstract collages and landscapes. All of her work reflects her many years of watercolor painting.

Dawn has also been an art educator for over 25 years. For the past 15, she's focused on providing art-related programming for the elderly and those living with dementia.

Dawn and her art can be found online at dawnrozzo.com.

About the Author

Originally from Iowa, Karin Wiberg now lives in Raleigh, North Carolina, where she helps business professionals write and publish books. Her poetry has been published in *Two Hawks Quarterly*, *Stirring*, *riverSedge*, and elsewhere.

When not tending to clients or chickens, Karin can be found reading student essays for the Jane Austen Society of North America (JASNA) and the Phi Beta Kappa (PBK) Association of Wake County, or grant applications for the Office of Raleigh Arts and the North Carolina Arts Council.

Karin holds an MBA from the University of Iowa and a BA from Gustavus Adolphus. She can be found online at clearsightbooks.com and karinwiberg.com.